M000014870

To:

_____

From:

_____

Date:

_____

Message:

_____

_____

_____

Just a Taste of Honey

Norine Rendall

MOODY
The Name You Can Trust®
A MINISTRY OF MOODY BIBLE INSTITUTE

JUST A TASTE OF HONEY by Norline Rendall

© 1999:   Christian Art
            PO Box 1599
            Vereeniging
            1930
            South Africa

This book was first published in the United States by Moody Press with
the title of *Just a Taste of Honey*, copyright © 1975 by the Moody Bible
Institute of Chicago.

Designed by: Christian Art

ISBN 08024-4756-2

Printed in Singapore.

Taste a little honey

Bible Reading: Proverbs 24:13-14

It was in my mouth as honey for sweetness.
Ezekiel 3:3

The story is told of Samuel L. Brengle walking into a New York office on a stifling, humid day. As he approached the chic secretary, he mopped his brow and implored her to tell him how to keep cool.

Ignoring his question under the weight of her own problem, she begged, "I wish someone would tell me how to keep sweet."

Obviously she had been facing situations that continually brought out the worst in her. One can imagine her resolutions day after day as she came to work. She would not let the lazy janitor upset her. She would not get so annoyed with the salesman who was always having to phone back for something he had forgotten. She would be patient with her boss when he was just too fussy. She would not snap back at persistently complaining and demanding customers.

But each day ended the same. Not in one instance was she able to act like the person she wanted to be. Short, snappy words and miserable looks and actions plagued her.

More than she wanted the physical comfort of relief from extreme heat, she wanted the inner assurance that she as a person could handle each minute sweetly and calmly.

We have an answer to our personality problems. We have a source of sweetness that we can draw on. The psalmist in 119:103 declares, "How sweet are thy words unto my taste! yea, sweeter than honey to my mouth!"

As we daily feed upon God's Word, we can become more like Him. His sweetness will be evident in our lives as each day we taste a little honey.

We don't forget;
we just don't do it!

Bible Reading: James 4:13-17

Therefore to him that knoweth to do good,
and doeth it not, to him it is sin (v. 17).

It was a cold, blustery winter day. Since I was sick in bed, my husband was doing his best to act as nursemaid and baby sitter. Feeling equal to the task, he suggested to the boys that he help straighten their room.

Now, there was one main problem: our children are born collectors. It doesn't really matter how worthless the item is. It can be stones that *might* be pretty if they were cracked open, pictures that *might* be needed someday, discarded bolts, nuts, screws, wire, or bent rusty nails. Each suggests some potential project in their little minds.

As I lay listening to the noises and voices coming from the other bedroom, I had to smile in spite of an aching head and burning throat. The comments were so familiar. I had said to them many times: "Why are you keeping this?" "This is just junk!" "You have to get rid of some of this stuff." "You must keep your room neater." "Put your clothes where they belong." "Put each toy in its proper place." And so on.

After an impressive heap had been labeled "garbage," it was time for bedtime stories.

Just as though it had been planned, the story began, "Keith could never remember to do the things he was supposed to do. He forgot to –" At this my husband paused. "It sounds like someone else had trouble remembering the things he was supposed to do."

"Oh," piped up Stevie, then seven years old. "We don't forget; we just don't do it."

What a revelation! If only we adults had the honesty of this boy! If only we would admit that we don't have any excuse for some of the things we neglect to do! Too often we simply don't bother doing them. They may take a little time, a little effort, but we fail to put it forth. We know better.

God's Word has a more serious label for our neglect. He tells us that not doing what we know we should do is sinning. What are we going to do about it?

Wisdom for our work

Bible Reading: Exodus 35:30-35

Them hath he filled with wisdom of heart, to work all manner of work, of the engraver, and of the cunning workman, and of the embroiderer, in blue, and in purple, in scarlet, and in fine linen, and of the weaver, even of them that do any work, and of those that devise cunning work (v. 35).

J had been doing a considerable amount of sewing. Somehow these jobs manage to pile up nearly every spring: sewing for the family, making gifts for relatives and friends, struggling with the ever-increasing pile of mending. Sew, sew, sew.

It all is very necessary, but at times one starts wishing there were more time for something that would last a little longer. You know how it is. You mend, but soon the buttons are off again; the knees are worn through.

You wash and iron clothes just to see the same ones back again next time, ready for the same round. You dust and clean, but what is the use? Everything needs it again the next day.

So I was pretty pleased to read our scripture portion for today, especially verse 35. Those men who cut the patterns, sewed the seams, and added the finishing touches were filled with the Spirit of God for their job. Those who carved wood and cut stone also needed God's help. These were their God-given tasks. No matter how mundane, God supplied them with wisdom for it.

Maybe it is hard to comprehend how God can be interested in the daily tasks of life; but if He gave wisdom to the workers in Moses' day, surely He will give wisdom to us for our work. We can *know* we are serving Him in performing our daily duties.

> *The task Thy wisdom hath assigned*
> *O let me cheerfully fulfil;*
> *In all my works Thy presence find,*
> *And prove Thy good and perfect will.*
> *~ Charles Wesley ~*

Dead or alive?

Bible Reading: John 15:1-6

Abide in me, and I in you. As the branch
cannot bear fruit of itself, except it abide in the
vine; no more can ye except ye abide in me (v. 4).

Our family was vacationing at a crude cabin in the
woods. It certainly didn't have any of the luxuries of
modern-day living, but it was a welcome change from
the daily grind.

All of us enjoyed walking among the trees, feeding
the squirrels with the nuts we had brought along for this
purpose, spotting the large variety of birds, and picking
handfuls of wild flowers.

But the flowers I liked best were the Alberta wild roses.
What a delightful fragrance they gave; what a delicate
color and design they had! Time-and-time again we
picked a bouquet of these dainty flowers, carefully

arranged them in an old teapot, and sat back to enjoy their beauty.

But not for long. Soon the petals began to fall, and the leaves began to wither. What was wrong? Why did they look so bedraggled so soon? The answer was simple. They were no longer connected to their lifegiving plant. For a few hours they could put up a pretty good show, but soon the truth came out. They were dead.

There are people about us who are spiritually dead; they have never enjoyed spiritual life as it is found in Christ. We can readily tell that. But by a divine miracle of salvation they can have Christ's life within them. By asking the Lord Jesus into their hearts, they can have sustaining spiritual life.

What about those of us who are attached to this life-giving source? Can others see Christ living in us? Is it evident that we belong to Him and are letting His beauty and blessing flow through us? According to our Saviour in John 15, we may enjoy this abiding relationship with Him by keeping His commandments.

I am praying, blessed Savior,
And my constant prayer shall be,
For a perfect consecration,
That shall make me more like Thee.
~ Fanny J. Crosby ~

Second~mile patience

Bible Reading: Matthew 5:41-48

*And whosoever shall compel thee to
go a mile, go with him twain (v. 41).*

$\mathcal{B}$efore I became a full-time housewife, I worked
occasionally as a telephone operator. And I'll assure you
that being a telephone operator can make you want to
scream!

Although an operator tries to do her best to keep sweet
and patient even with demanding customers, sometimes
it is hard. There is the day when nothing goes right, and
her customers are quick to tell her. It seems that every
number she dials ends up with a busy signal or a pro-
longed ringing, indicating that the party wanted is not
in. And then, when she finally manages to get through,
she learns she has dialed the wrong number!

I was reading about such an operator. After completing a call, she remarked to her fellow-operator: "What a patient man! I was flustered and gave him the wrong number *four times*. When he called back the fifth time, he still sounded patient and quietly asked if I would try again. I'd like to meet a man like that."

The second operator in an attempt to identify the unusual customer, asked what his number was. Upon being told, she exclaimed, "Oh, I know him! He is my minister!"

"Then, I'm going to hear him preach next Sunday!" concluded the impressed operator.

Don't you think it was probably difficult to remain patient and kind – at least by the third time the minister received the wrong number? I don't think it was. I believe this servant of God was practising the life he lived from day to day. He believed in second-mile patience, in second-mile service, no matter what sphere it affected.

Going the first mile is not uncommon or unusual, but it is our second-mile service that is a practical testimony of our Christianity.

Help me to stay home

Bible Reading: 1 John 5:11-15

*If we ask any thing according
to his will, he heareth us (v. 14).*

$\mathcal{J}$ was having bedtime devotions with our boys. After reading their Bible story for the evening, we began discussing prayer requests. Then I mentioned that the younger had to go to the doctor the following day and suggested we pray for a safe trip for the two hundred miles we needed to travel.

Without hesitation and with all earnestness our five-year-old began, "Dear Lord Jesus, help me to stay home. Amen."

I suppressed a grin and began to explain that God answers our prayers in three ways: Sometimes He says, "Yes, you may have what you ask for"; sometimes He says, "No, I don't want you to have your request"; and sometimes it is simply, "Wait, it is not time yet for you to have your answer."

And surely enough the answer to this little boy's prayer was "No," largely because he asked according to his own desires.

What about our prayers? Do we pray, "Thy will be done," and "Please give me strength and courage to do Thy will whatever it is"? Or do we selfishly pray for what we want the way we want it, without any thought about what God has for us?

God hasn't promised to answer all our prayers affirmatively. But He has promised to answer all our prayers that are prayed with His will as our strongest desire.

Approach, my soul, the mercy seat,
Where Jesus answers prayer;
There humbly fall before His feet,
For none can perish there.

Thy promise is my only plea,
With this I venture nigh;
Thou callest burdened souls to Thee,
And such, O Lord, am I!
~ John Newton ~

The well of the heart

Bible Reading: Philippians 4:8-9

Whatsoever things are true, whatsoever things are honest, whatsoever things are just, whatsoever thing are pure, whatsoever things are lovely, whatsoever things are of good report; if there be any virtue, and if there be any praise, think on these things (v. 8).

At our student testimony meeting I heard one of our students telling the following. Before he was saved he had thought he had no need of a Saviour. He had wondered if and how Christians were different from other people. But gradually one specific man began having an influence on him. Was it really possible to live all the time the life this man was living?

Then the test came. The Christian man was repairing his car engine. He straightened up very quickly and gave his head a mighty whack. Now, what would he say?

Would he go into a rage and use bad language?

The Christian didn't say a word. He kept quiet and after a moment continued his work in spite of a pounding head.

So that was it! This man didn't let off a stream of curse words. He didn't get angry or call the car names. This was a difference the student couldn't explain. He was so impressed that eventually he came to find Christ as his Saviour and Redeemer from sin, too. If Christ could make such a difference in the life of his friend, then Christ was the One he needed.

Others are watching us, watching the kind of lives we live. Is there any visible difference between our reactions and the reactions of someone who doesn't belong to Christ. There are plenty of everyday opportunities that we can take to be a witness and testimony for Christ. Not always will it be the words we speak; it may be the words we don't speak or the things we don't do that will influence someone for Christ.

The proverb states it well: "What is in the well of the heart comes up in the bucket of speech."

Let us ask God to fill our hearts full of the fruit of the Spirit. Then when we are jolted, only His goodness can spill out to others.

Look for the best!

Bible Reading: Matthew 7:1-5

Judge not, that ye be not judged. For with what judgment ye judge, ye shall be judged (vv. 1-2).

My husband brought home a children's book he wanted me to read to our boys. But before I read it aloud, I read snatches of it here and there and soon put it down, convinced that it was a poorly written book with a dull plot.

A few days later I began reading the book to our sons, a chapter an evening. Before many nights had passed, I found myself sending them on to bed while I curled up in a comfortable chair, absorbed in this same children's book – and I read it to the end, fascinated.

Then a sense of guilt flooded me. Wasn't this the book I had quickly glanced through only long enough to form a negative opinion? Wasn't this the book I was reading to my children simply because we had finished the previous book?

If we do that with books, what about people? It is easy to form an opinion of someone from a few brief meetings. The fact is, we are seeing only glimpses of them; many of their good qualities are hidden from the casual observer.

Or maybe we form some false conclusion based on gossip we hear. If only we took time to gather all the facts before forming an opinion and passing it on, a lot of embarrassment would be avoided.

May God help us to look for the best in people. After all, if His love for us depended on our own merits, we would all be forsaken.

Sweet snare

Bible Reading: Colossians 3:1-4

*Set your affection [mind] on things
above, not on things on the earth (v. 2).*

$\mathcal{B}$efore we went away for a few days I purchased, along with other groceries, a bag of sugar. After I filled the cannister, there was a cup of sugar left in the bag, so I rolled up the bag and left it out on the kitchen counter.

When we returned home, I opened the bag to use the sugar and discovered a dead fly. The sweetness inside the bag had apparently been a strong enough attraction to cause the fly to work its way round and round the folds until it reached the contents. But alas! The fly could not live on sweetness alone, and escape out of the "sweet trap" must have seemed too much for it. It died in the midst of sweetness.

Sometimes we are like this fly. We struggle and strive to achieve something, to get somewhere, to earn a position, to acquire possessions – only to be suffocated by the very thing that has attracted us.

Or there may be some "sweet sin" luring us away from that which is right. For the moment it looks so good, so lovely, so satisfying. But look out! It is deadly!

Let us resolve not to be influenced by the world and its attractions. The joy thus brought is short-lived and unworthy of the effort required to achieve it. The sweetness is only a snare to get us involved. Escape now while there is still a chance!

> *O, let me feel Thee near me,*
> *The world is ever near;*
> *I see the sights that dazzle,*
> *The tempting sounds I hear.*
> *My foes are ever near me,*
> *Around me and within;*
> *But, Jesus, draw Thou nearer,*
> *And shield my soul from sin.*
> *~ John E. Bode ~*

ℐ found it!

Bible Reading: 2 Chronicles 34:14-18

*Thy words were found, and I did eat
them; and thy word was unto me
the joy and rejoicing of mine heart.*
Jeremiah 15:16

𝒯hree-year old Stevie really treasured his New Testament. But one day he couldn't find it. I knew it had to be in the house, but where?

My only complaint about having a tidy house is the frustration one feels when something goes astray. If there are places that need tidying, it doesn't seem so hopeless. There is always a chance of finding the lost article there!

But that day our house was in order, and I didn't know a place where the New Testament could stay lost.

Days passed. The little Book simply couldn't be found.

And then while I was hanging some freshly laundered clothes in the boy's closet and Stevie was playing around at my feet, I heard a happy shout, "I found it!" And surely enough, he had found his Bible inside an empty suitcase stored in the closet!

Stevie's Bible is not the only one that has been lost. In 2 Chronicles 34 we read that the Book of the Law had been misplaced. Josiah's men uncovered it stowed away in the temple.

Where is your Bible? In the cupboard? On the shelf? Displayed on the table? Is it neglected, or are you making daily use of it?

Let us shout, "I found it!" Not in the literal sense of having found the material Bible but of having discovered for ourselves the hidden truths contained therein.

Then we can exclaim with Jeremiah, "Thy words were found, and I did eat them; and thy word was unto me the joy and rejoicing of mine heart."

Thanks for the Bible, offering so freely
Pardon and peace to all who believe.
Help us, O Lord, its counsel to follow,
Meekly by faith its truth to receive.
~ Fanny J. Crosby ~

Add a little honey

Bible Reading: Psalm 19:1-14

Pleasant words are as an honeycomb,
sweet to the soul, and health to the bones.
Proverbs 16:24

The boys were imploring me to make a batch of ice cream. Looking at the clock, I decided there was just time to make it and have it ready to serve for supper.

With interruptions and instructions from the boys, I put the ingredients together. In the course of time the ice cream was declared ready, and the boys were discussing who would get the dasher and who would get to clean out the container.

Lifting the lid carefully so that no salty ice would slip inside, we saw the beautifully fluffy ice cream. One of the boys exclaimed that it looked so good he was sure he could eat it all. I emptied most of the ice cream into a large bowl and let the boys clean off the rest.

After a couple of licks one of the kids screwed up his nose and sputtered, "Ugh! Taste it, Mom." I did and nearly wished I hadn't. Have you ever tried peppermint ice cream without any sweetening added? I don't recommend it!

How could anything look so good and taste so bad? After all, all the other ingredients were there; only one had been omitted. But it just couldn't be eaten that way. Sweetness had to be added before the ice cream could be enjoyed by anyone.

Do our lives look pretty good from a distance? Those who see us only at church or on social occasions may not realize how our tongues can cut those with whom we work or live. These with whom we associate most closely are the ones who well know if a very important ingredient – one that will make us palatable as it were – is missing.

Add a little honey; a little sweetness may make all the difference.

I could stop and cry

Bible Reading: Romans 12:9-15

Rejoice with them that do rejoice,
and weep with them that weep (v. 15).

Seven-year-old Mary was late getting home from school. Her worried mother immediately questioned her. "Whatever kept you so long? Did you have to stay in to finish some work? Why are you late?"

"Oh, you see," replied Mary softly, "Susie dropped her doll, and it broke into five pieces."

"I don't understand why this should make you late in getting home. Were you trying to help Susie fix her doll?"

"Oh, no, Mom. I could never fix Susie's doll. It is too broken. But I could stop and cry with her. It was much better than her being sad all alone."

If we are alert, we can find people who need us to

forget ourselves, our schedule, our pleasures, long enough to do some crying with them. Often we are at a loss to mend the circumstances which cause our friends' hearts to be heavy. We cannot restore to them their loved one whom they have lost; we cannot heal their broken and wounded bodies; we cannot rebuild their destroyed homes.

But we can sympathize with them. We can let them know that their sorrow is our sorrow, too. We can listen to them understandingly and patiently, thus helping to relieve the burden that has weighed so heavily upon them. We can share with them verses from God's Word, given to us by the Great comforter.

We may not have great talents, but if we have a sympathetic heart and a listening ear, God can use us to the blessing, help, and comfort of others.

Believe it: God is interested

Bible Reading: Matthew 10:29-33

Be careful for nothing; but in every thing by prayer and supplication with thanksgiving let your requests be made known unto God.
Philippians 4:6

The death of my washing machine was announced by the smell of smoke. The motor had burned out. So week after week found me spending the best part of half a day doing our wash at the laundry.

But when friends were moving away and offered to sell their machine for five dollars (because they couldn't guarantee how long it might run), I didn't hesitate. Even if it would do our washing for a few weeks, I reasoned, it would be worth it.

So Saturday evening found me loading this machine for the second time. I started turning buttons and dials, but it simply refused to start. Was it finished?

Finally, I left it to get on with another job. All the time I was silently praying that somehow the washer would run, even just long enough to get through this particular load.

And then I had the growing conviction that I should pray definitely that it would start. I told my husband, and together we walked to the machine. We prayed. Now what? I really didn't know.

"Well," I said, "you take that side, and I'll take this. And we'll push and pull all the knobs we can find."

The light flickered, and water began pouring into the tub. I felt an immense relief that my washing problem for that night had been solved. But even greater was my gratitude to our loving heavenly Father. He was interested in this little detail of life. He had been pleased to answer prayer. "Thank You, Lord," I remember to say.

Overlooking the easy

Bible Reader: Mark 5:18-20

Whatsoever thy hand findeth
to do, do it with thy might.
Ecclesiastes 9:10

We had just moved to the house across the street. It wasn't a long move, to be sure, but perhaps more backbreaking than the usual move where you use a truck to move the boxes instead of packing them across the street one-by-one.

Anyway, we were nearly settled. The house we had left was empty, but we still had some items in the yard. So I asked our boys, seven and eight, to bring over a few of the smaller toys and tools. I emphasized that they should not try to move the large tractor tire which had served as their sandbox.

Ten minutes later I looked out the window to see how they were getting along. Having forgotten completely about the hoe, rake, bicycle, and other items that could be easily moved, they were struggling in an effort to move the tire. They tried everything they could think of but could not budge it more than a few inches.

As I watched the boys from the window, I realized that they were so typical of us older human beings! They were wasting their energy and time on a task far too big for them and neglecting the jobs they were told to do and were able to do.

We attempt – and fail – to fill the most impressive positions, and shun the lowly behind-the-scene jobs God asks us to take on. We long for spectacular opportunities that require talents we do not have, rather than use the talents God has given us to do simple daily tasks.

Let's take up the work available now that we are able to do. No job that is done in loving obedience to God is considered unimportant by Him. Perhaps He will use it to prepare us for greater service in the future.

If done to obey Thy laws,
E'en servile labors shine;
Hallowed is toil, if this the cause,
The meanest work, divine.
~ George Herbert ~

Spitting out forgiveness

Bible Reading: Mark 11:24-26

*Forgive, if ye have ought against any;
that your Father also which is in Heaven
may forgive you your trespasses (v. 25).*

*U*nfortunately, I had missed the earlier part of their conversation. Obviously they had had a fight or at least a heated argument about something.

Anyway, what I did hear stopped me in my tracks.

The older child was saying, "The Lord loves forgiving souls. Do you forgive me?"

The younger put his tongue out and spat, "I said, 'Yes.'" And there was some more spitting, and that little red tongue popped out again.

Even though it sounded like a rather serious occasion, I could barely keep from snickering. Here this little lad was saying that he was forgiving the older one, but no one could tell it either by his sounds or his actions!Often children are unafraid to show how they really feel about something or someone. We adults, on the other hand, do our best to put on a good front. If someone comes to us and asks forgiveness for a wrong done, it is only proper that we say we forgive them.

But it is possible that within we still hold a grudge. We still remember that so and so did such and such to us at one time. We let it color our thinking, let it actually affect our relationship with him.

Do we want our Lord to forgive us to the same degree as we forgive others?

More about Jesus would I know,
More of His grace to others show;
More of His saving fulness see,
More of His love – who died for me.
~ E.E. Hewitt ~

Mommie said

Bible Reading: Numbers 32:20-23

Be sure your sin will find you out (v. 23).

*F*or a number of days I had been wondering how true were the words spoken by the little girl who lived down the street. Periodically she would knock persistently at the door. And when I answered, it was always, "Mommie said –" Perhaps it was, "Mommie said it would be all right if I got my swimming suit on and ran through your sprinkler," or "Mommie said it would be all right if you gave me a cookie."

That is, I wondered until one cold, cloudy spring day. It was a perfect day for baking, which I was doing, when again I heard the familiar knock. "Maybe she smells the cookies," I thought as I walked to the door."

"Yes, Nellie, what would you like today?"

"Mommie said I can run through the sprinkler if you will turn it on."

The past incidents became absolutely clear. Mommie would no more want her four-year-old to run through cold water on a dreary drizzly day than I would have wanted her to. This time I wasn't going to give in and stated firmly, "No, you tell your mommie it is too cold."

This incident reminds me of our scripture verse for today. Nellie had probably got into the habit of lying gradually. Perhaps I had even encouraged it. She soon discovered that all she had to say was "Mommie said," and everything went as she wanted. But finally the time came when the lie was so obvious that even I could detect it!

Are we always absolutely truthful in what we say? Or do we find ourselves beginning to shade statements just a wee bit and then a bit more? Look out! Some day the sin of lying will find us out. Let us ask God to keep our every statement absolutely truthful.

To Thy cross I cling

Bible Reading: John 3:14-21

*Not by works of righteousness which we
have done, but according to his mercy
he saved us, by the washing of regene-
ration, and renewing of the Holy Ghost.*
Titus 3:5

$\mathcal{J}$ had just come home from attending the funeral service
for a sweet, vibrant Christian lady. Her life had simply
radiated the love of our Lord Jesus Christ.

At the close of the services, we paused to speak with
the bereaved husband. As we chatted with him, he told
us how she had suffered a massive brain hemorrhage
while he was helping feed her breakfast one morning.

He went on to tell us that when she had been told that
she had a fatal disease and only a short time left to live,
she had tearfully looked up into the face of her partner

and exclaimed, "I have so little to give Him."

Before he could answer, from down the hospital hall on someone's radio or television a soloist burst forth singing, "Nothing in my hand I bring; simply to Thy Cross I cling." She was comforted, happy in the knowledge that Jesus was all she needed.

Living for the Lord and doing His work are very necessary aspects of being a Christian, but they don't bring us salvation. Only as we trust in the finished work of Jesus Christ on the cross can we face death triumphantly.

> *Not the labors of my hands*
> *Can fulfil Thy law's demands:*
> *Could my zeal no respite know,*
> *Could my tears for ever flow,*
> *All for sin could not atone;*
> *Thou must save, and Thou alone.*
>
> *Nothing in my hand I bring,*
> *Simply to Thy Cross I cling;*
> *Naked, come to Thee for dress;*
> *Helpless, look to Thee for grace;*
> *Foul, I to the fountain fly;*
> *Wash me, Saviour, or I die.*
> *~ Augustus M. Toplady ~*

It's growing

Bible Reading: 2 Peter 3:14-18

*But grow in grace, and in the knowledge of
our Lord and Saviour Jesus Christ (v. 18).*

I had delayed giving permission as long as possible.
Our seven-year-old was asking to go out on this muddy
day and bring in some soil so he could plant a few seeds.
Being unable to think of any more distractions or
excuses, I reluctantly gave my permission, cringing at
my mental picture of a muddy jar, muddy hands, muddy
boots, and muddy clothes.

To my surprise he returned to the house with his jar
partially filled with soil, but not a trace of mud to be
seen. He must have found a protected spot of garden!
Frankly, I was amazed. I probably wouldn't have done
so well!

The seeds were planted, and he watered them generously. In a few days I heard Davie dancing gaily through the house. Into the kitchen he burst, bubbling, "I am *so* happy."

"Why, dear? Why are you happy?"

"It is growing! My plant is growing. I am *so* happy!" And he skipped out.

It is difficult to find anyone who doesn't enjoy spring with its sudden new growth. Who doesn't feel exuberant walking up a street lined with freshly leaved trees, or thrilled seeing new shoots growing in the flower bed and the tiny sprouts in the vegetable garden?

As I thought of the happiness brought to us by growing, living plants, I thought of the gardener of our souls. Can He exclaim, "She is growing! I am *so* happy!" After He has tenderly provided for our needs, cared for us, and watched over us, can He see any growth for His efforts?

Holidays and heaven

Bible Reading: Matthew 6:19-21

To be with Christ; which is far better.
Philippians 1:23

Everybody was talking about holidays! And we were no exception. For a few years we had been planning a special vacation, a long-dreamed of trip to Scotland, my husband's native land.

There had been one goal before us. Months of saving and planning had gone into preparations. No sacrifice was too great if only we could go! Many travel agencies had been contacted; maps had been pored over; catalogs had been memorized.

It was a long-awaited trip. Everything had to be just right. Wardrobes had to be planned and chosen with care so that the least would do the most! Lists had been drawn up and added to. It wouldn't do to leave behind even one essential article.

Sewing, making, remaking – every item had to fit just right, look just right, and match a certain number of accessories to be eligible to go.

Daily life had been centered around this important event. In fact, at times that is all we could talk about! Sometimes I was quite sure my friends would be glad when we had made the trip!

As we planned and packed, I was conscious of all the effort, time, and money that was going into this holiday. Then my mind strayed beyond this earth and its needs and pleasures, and I began wondering if as much preparation was going into the trip to heaven we know we shall take some day.

Do we long to see Christ with as much anticipation as we have for our earthly loved ones? With our passage having been booked (the Lord Jesus Christ bought the ticket), are we now sending ahead an outfit that we shall be pleased to wear in heaven? Our holidays, no matter how exciting, are insignificant in comparison to our coming journey to heaven! Let us give it the preparation it deserves.

Of leopards and angels

Bible Reading: Psalm 34:1-8

The angel of the Lord encampeth round about them that fear him, and delivereth them (v. 7).

From time to time it is our privilege to entertain men of God who come to minister His Word at Prairie Bible Institute. At one of our spring conferences Dr. Lionel Gurney was our dinner guest. A vivid story teller, he was encouraged to tell story after story to satisfy the requests of one of our sons. One incident, especially, we will not forget, and I would like to share it with you.

In a Muslim country a young girl named Ama was sent on an errand to the next village. The errand took longer than was expected, and Ama found herself returning home through the forest after dark. At last she was near enough home that she felt she could relax a bit

– until suddenly she realized that a leopard was circling her.

Young though she was Ama knew the dangers. She well-knew that leopards never leave a prey once they start stalking it. Too frightened to go farther, Ama sat on the ground and earnestly prayed to the Lord Jesus whom she had learned to trust. All the time the leopard was circling closer and closer. Then it walked up to the child, lay down beside her, put its head in her lap, and purred. Eventually, it got up and disappeared into the woods.

As soon as Ama had gathered the strength, she stood to her feet and made her way home. She was too frightened to mention this experience to her father until a month later. It was then her Muslim father admitted that, the very night of which his daughter was speaking, he had smelled a leopard and had feared for her life but had said nothing. Ama told her father that she had prayed to the true God, and He had answered her prayer. Her father couldn't deny that God alone could have answered in such a miraculous way.

Is there something upsetting or frightening you? As a child of God you have every right to pray for His protection and care. Then trust Him.

Crabby Christians
and shoddy saints

Bible Reading: 1 Peter 2:1-10

*But ye are a chosen generation, ... that ye should
shew forth the praises of him who hath called you
out of darkness into his marvellous light (v. 9).*

Prairie is a license-plate watcher's paradise! In any
given year it is possible to see cars with license plates
that advertise New Brunswick, Ontario, Manitoba,
Wisconsin, South Carolina, Connecticut, California,
Texas, Wa-shington, etc.

While walking through campus, we noticed a well-
used vehicle parked outside the dining room. Not only
was it beat-up and badly in need of a new paint job, but
also it was muddy from top to bottom. Through the grime

one could barely detect the writing on the license plate, "Beautiful British Columbia."

Beautiful British Columbia – but one would never imagine the beauties of that province by looking at the car! The automobile was definitely not a sample of the province's scenery!

How about us? Do we bear the name Christian on our lives that won't draw anyone to Christ? Do we claim the name but leave our lives so cluttered with cares of this life that we are not an effective testimony to those with whom we come in contact daily?

A shoddy appearance won't attract anyone to the One we love and serve. A gloomy countenance won't advertise our Saviour, who gives joy and peace. An ugly disposition won't make people want what we have.

Let us bear the name Christian proudly and on a product that will advertise the delight of belonging to Christ.

Forth in Thy name, O Lord, I go,
My daily labor to pursue;
Thee, only Thee, resolved to know
In all I think, or speak, or do.
~ Charles Wesley ~

Skates, spuds, and soap

Bible Reading: Philippians 4:10-14, 17-19

But my God shall supply all your need according to his riches in glory by Christ Jesus (v. 19).

Nancy and her husband were engaged in full-time Christian service. They knew what it was to trust God for the supply of everyday needs.

But this month there had been added expenses, and as Nancy went about her housework, she was conscious that the Lord was going to have to do something unusual for them. She had four dollars left with which to buy groceries for the two weeks that remained.

That very noon a knock came on the door. "Could your son wear these skates? Our boy has outgrown them."

They fitted her son perfectly and looked like new.

In the afternoon Nancy went to the store. Potatoes topped her brief list. She was starting to put a few in a small paper bag when a friend walked by. "You need potatoes? I'll bring you a hundred pounds of big ones!"

With a happy heart Nancy walked to the soap counter but couldn't bring herself to buy any soap. After all, she did have enough for a couple more loads of clothes, although she well knew that this wouldn't take care of their washing for the remainder of the month.

Singing silent praises for the promised bag of potatoes, Nancy returned home. What was that on her doorstep? A medium-sized box of soap? But why? Where had it come from? Upon picking it up, she read "Sample Box," and a very generous sample it was! So this was why the Lord hadn't let her buy soap at the store. She didn't need any!

Nancy rejoiced. Skates, spuds, soap – all in one day, supplied by a loving heavenly Father. They were His children. He was caring for them as He had promised.

Drink milk!

Bible Reading: 2 Timothy 3:12-17

All scripture is given by inspiration of God, and is profitable for doctrine, for reproof, for correction, for instruction in righteousness (v. 16).

Remember the health posters we made in school? It seems that this is one phase of school life which has remained unchanged!

One day our first grader came home asking that we help him find a picture of milk. He was making a poster. It took a good deal of looking! Fruit, vegetables, cookies, candies, cakes, pies – you name it; food pictures were scattered throughout the magazines except for pictures of milk. But finally a picture of a glass of milk was found, and Davie ran off to school with it.

I had forgotten about our frantic search until the day

he brought his poster home. It proved to be very simple, just a glass of milk encircled with the words DRINK MILK. Proudly he showed it to me, and before I realized it he was attaching it to the refrigerator door with tape. True, it didn't add much to the decor, but I was sure the tape would soon dry up or that some accident would befall the poster which would give me a good excuse for removing it.

But the tape didn't dry, and no one bumped the poster to tear it! It remained unmoved until one day Davie left half a glass of milk at the dinner table. I reminded him of his poster. "You will have to drink your milk. See what the poster says."

"Then I'll have to take it down, because I don't want to drink my milk," as though taking the poster down would alter the facts!"

We might be able to excuse a child for this kind of reasoning, but I have heard of adults who feel this way about the Bible, the Word of God. If a certain verse or passage doesn't agree with their way of living and thinking, then they want to remove it. Or they simply state that it doesn't belong in the Bible.

God has given us His Word for a purpose. Let us happily obey it!

Fortitude in trouble

Bible Reading: Hebrews 13:5-9

*So that we may boldly say, the Lord is my helper,
and I will not fear what man shall do unto me (v. 6).*

$\mathcal{A}$ former classmate dropped in for coffee. We hadn't seen each other for years and found much to talk about.

As we chatted, Clara mentioned that, besides keeping house for her family, she was taking night classes in sociology. She then related her experience.

"The discussion under religion was extremely negative. One girl said there was no God, and if there was, He was only for the weak-minded. One older man said it was a crutch, and so on.

"After class I had reason to speak with my professor. She asked me if I had not felt that the discussion on religion was very negative. 'Yes', I told her, 'but I was too shy in class to speak up.' Anyway, she laughingly said, 'Next week I'll expect a sermon from you.' Although she had said it in fun, I could not get the idea out of my head, and so I began praying for wisdom to say the right words if she really did call on me.

"On the day of our evening class I felt sick. I resisted the devil and told him I would go to class anyway and speak up for the Lord. Just like that my illness left me.

"Our professor soon had the discussion back to where we had left off. Then she called my name. I said that I considered it a privilege to believe in God and Jesus Christ. And such words as peace, forgiveness of sins, removal of guilt, eternal life, prayer, and answers to prayer were words with daily meaning to me. Maybe then I should be counted among the weakminded!

"But my professor disagreed (Praise the Lord, I had made an A+ in my exam), and added, 'You probably have more fortitude in the face of trouble than others'."

People around us may not accept the truths of Christianity, but they do expect professing believers to be different. It is our reponsibility as Christ's disciples to witness boldly to our faith.

Honey out of the rock

Bible Reading: Romans 8:28-31

He made him ride on the high places of
the earth, that he might eat the increase of
the fields; and he made him to suck honey
out of the rock, and oil out of the flinty rock.
Deuteronomy 32:13

I had made arrangements for a young couple coming to school to rent an apartment for the term. They came to see the apartment, and as far as they and I were concerned, everything was settled.

But through a series of unpredictable circumstances it turned out that the apartment was no longer available. Even though I was confident that the Lord had a reason for allowing this, I was somewhat troubled. The beginning of school was quickly approaching, and the students would arrive and learn that they had nowhere to live.

After praying about the matter, I did some phoning and some looking. All the suitable apartments were booked. Just nothing livable was available. Daily I prayed that the Lord would work a miracle.

Eventually the couple had to learn of their dilemma. On the morning of the day the fellow was to arrive, I heard that one of our friends had decided to build an apartment in his spacious basement.

That afternoon we drove to the house. The work they had already done was evidence that this was the apartment we were looking for. It turned out to be exactly what our couple needed, really a great deal more suitable than the one they had lost.

Yes, those days of wondering and looking and waiting were hard. They were a strain. I felt so responsible to find something suitable when it seemed absolutely nothing was available. But the Lord gave us "honey out of the rock." He caused the impossible circumstances to bring forth good. The second apartment had many advantages over the first.

Rocks, hard things, impossible situations – the Lord wants to use them all for His glory. He will bring us good in and out of the hard places.

Look Up!

Bible Reading: Psalm 5:1-3

*My voice shalt thou hear in the morning,
O Lord; in the morning will I direct my
prayer unto thee, and will look up (v. 3).*

The postcards are right: the beauty of the Swiss Alps is simply breath-taking. To me the whole countryside resembles a well-kept, cultivated parkland with flower-decked chalets and rustic mountain huts sprinkled here and there to add an atmosphere of their own.

But as we drove along, we came to a mountain road which was very frightening; high mountain peaks were on one side and deep, deep gorges on the other. In true European style we zoomed around one sharp corner after another – all on a dangerously narrow road with no guard railings. At this particular time the canyon was on the right side where I was sitting. I felt sure we would slide over the edge!

Stevie felt me shudder as the situation worsened. He whispered, "Don't look down, Mommie. Look up!"

He may have been thinking of all the glorious beauty about us and above us that I was missing by concentrating on the dangers below. But I got the message. This was a time to exercise complete trust in the protection of my loving heavenly Father rather than committing the day to Him and then worrying about every corner before us. Why look down at the circumstances when I could be looking up to Him for His care?

It may not be in the scenic Alps only that one can learn this lesson. Daily living presents many a situation where one is tempted to look down at the frustrations, discouragements, disappointments, whatever it may be, rather than looking up higher.

After we have committed our day to the Lord, let us not take our eyes off Him but continue to look up to Him no matter what the day may bring.

What's wrong with the bulb?

Bible Reading: Ephesians 2:1-10

For by grace are ye saved through faith; and that not of yourselves: it is the gift of God: Not of works, lest any man should boast (vv. 8,9).

*A*fter my husband had preached on the necessity of having the life of God in our hearts, a lady stopped at the door to tell him about a young relative of hers.

Four-year-old Linda was unusually fond of flowers and had overheard adults talking about planting bulbs. So after Christmas she secured a discarded light bulb, dug under the snow to fill her pot with soil, and carefully planted the bulb. Ever after, she faithfully watered the bulb and was bewildered because no growth was evident.

The grandma, who observed the child's disappointment, recently bought an amaryllis bulb for Linda to plant in exchange for the light bulb.

Now there is hope of growth! No matter how patiently the dead bulb would be cared for, there could never be growth – no life, no growth.

It is possible for us to wonder why there is no spiritual life evident in someone. Perhaps we need to check under the surface – under the top soil – to see from what source we are expecting this life to grow.

We may find a dead light bulb, a good-works effort. This will never produce spiritual growth. Salvation is needed. The life of Christ must be planted in a heart before growth can be evident.

"Ye must be born again!"
Then look to Christ, and live;
He is "the Life," and waits in heaven
Eternal life to give.
~ Albert Midlane ~

No place for me?

Bible Reading: Romans 12:16-21

*Let us therefore follow after the things
which make for peace, and things
wherewith one may edify another.*
Romans 14:19

Our Davie was a slow talker, but there was nothing wrong with his mathematical brain.

We had motored to the States for our summer holidays and at this particular time were visiting a childhood friend of mine.

Between her family and ours there were twelve of us, a full table at mealtime. After we had visited for several days, Donna prepared a delicious meal with all the trimmings as a special farewell for us.

She brought out her best china. I didn't bother counting as I set the table. I just took for granted that the right amount was there.

Davie had been watching me, and I could tell that something was upsetting him. But I had no way of knowing what. By the time everyone was called for dinner, he was really difficult to manage.

To make a long story short, two-and-a-half-year-old David had realized a place was missing and automatically had taken for granted that he was the one who was deliberately being left out. He was hurt as only a sensitive little boy who can't express his feelings can be.

Of course, no one intended that we be one place short. And certainly absolutely no one even thought of leaving out Davie. But *he* thought so!

Have we ever felt sorry for ourselves, convinced ourselves that someone was deliberately trying to overlook us or leave us out? Don't come to conclusions too fast! A legitimate mistake may have been made.

"Let us therefore follow after the things which make for peace" and forget those that lead to discord!

Do I have to smile?

Bible Reading: Psalm 146:1-10

Happy is he that hath the God of Jacob for his help, whose hope is in the Lord his God (v. 5).

We were entertaining a missionary from Holland. During the dinner hour he kept our boys listening attentively to his stories. Among others, he told them about his seven-year-old daughter. She is an avid tree climber; the higher the tree, the better she likes it!

Well, one day it happened. She fell from her elevated position to a crumpled heap on the ground. It was impossible for her parents to ascertain all her injuries, but it was obvious that both of her arms were broken. Carefully she was carried to the car and rushed to the hospital.

As she lay on the stretcher awaiting treatment, her

body was full of pain, and her heart was filling with fear. The uniformed attendant came along and told her that they were going to take an X ray (Roentgenphoto in Dutch). With tear-filled eyes and quavering lips, she whispered, "Do I have to smile?" Only the word "photo" (which means photograph) held any meaning for her.

We certainly do sympathize with this little girl and would ourselves find it difficult to pose with a smile in a similar condition. But I wonder how many of us simply don't want to smile when we are facing something unpleasant. We reserve our smiles only for the happy occasions, when smiling actually could help us be triumphant through many a difficulty.

Paul in writing to the Philippians in 4:4 tells them to "Rejoice in the Lord always: and again I say, Rejoice." Notice he is not conditioning his statement with favorable circumstances. "Always" means just that! In whatever situation you find yourself, try smiling. It helps!

Keep the door of my lips

Bible Reading: Psalm 141:1-10

Set a watch, O Lord, before my mouth;
keep the door of my lips (v. 3).

To the side of the road was a high bank of snow, piled there by the snowplow.

From the vantage point of our picture window, I watched six neighborhood children gather. One brought a toboggan. With effort they pulled the toboggan up over the slippery jagged edges until it teetered on the point, that is, until three children sat on it. Then it bent like a bow! As I held my breath, the oldest in the group gave a push from the rear.

One or two usually managed to slip right off the back as they headed straight down over the bumps. But what fun they were having! I could read it all over their faces, and a few times the louder peals of laughter penetrated our walls.

Fun, did I say? Only for a short while. As best as I could figure, one boy let go of the toboggan before he was supposed to, and a smaller fellow came along with an ugly protest. First, words flew, then chunks of snow, then fists. Finally, the younger boy, who appeared the fiercer fighter, received a blow he didn't appreciate and started crying.

The fight was over. But you could almost see a cloud forming over the children as they stood around. They had lost interest in their play, even the little ones who weren't directly involved in the tussle. Pretty soon a couple of the boys walked away. It just wasn't the same any longer.

It doesn't take very much to ruin a perfectly happy occasion. Just a few words spoken by someone who doesn't guard his tongue at that moment can ruin all the happiness and fellowship previously enjoyed. A few bitter, critical, or harsh words are all it takes to cause a cloud to hang over the entire gathering.

Let us make the psalmist's prayer our prayer: "Set a watch, O Lord, before my mouth; keep the door of my lips."

I'm not making a mess!

Bible Reading: 1 John 3:1-3

All things work together for good to
them that love God, to them who are
the called according to his purpose.
Romans 8:28

*A*nother washday! Somehow they have a way of turning up before a person has had a chance to recover from the last one.

As I entered our utility room with my arms piled high with a batch of laundry for the washing machine, I stumbled over block after block. There was our seven-year-old squatting contentedly among them.

Never having developed an appreciation for toys any place on the floor, let alone in the path of traffic, I blurted out, "Davie, what a mess you are making!"

66

His little blond head cocked indignantly, "I'm not making a mess! I'm building a garage." Upon closer examination I could distinguish in the middle of the scattered red blocks a building taking shape.

This was on a strictly human level, but I was quickly transported higher. Especially under the criticism of unsaved friends, are we sometimes tempted to feel that we could have made more of a success of our lives than what we have in our earnest attempts at following God's plan?

Cheer up! Perhaps at the moment we are surveying the scattered pieces with which God is building. Let's just trust Him!

Commit thou all thy griefs
And ways into His hands,
To His sure trust and tender care
Who earth and heaven commands.

Thy everlasting truth,
Father, Thy ceaseless love,
See all Thy children's wants, and knows
What best for each will prove.
~ Paul Gerhardt
~ Trans. John Wesley ~

Confidence or confusion?

Bible Reading: Isaiah 26:1-4

*In quietness and in confidence
shall be your strength.*
Isaiah 30:15

Right from the start, the day seemed like an impossibility. I was getting over the flu, had to type at least forty pages to meet an important deadline, and was going to have a meeting in our home that evening.

Before I could rub the sleep out of my eyes, the phone started ringing; and then callers started coming. Some had problems; others simply wanted to visit for a while. Inside I was becoming very restless, while endeavoring to maintain a calm appearance.

By noon only three or four pages were typed, and nothing had been done to the house. As I stood at the sink doing the dinner dishes, I was praying. Finally I told the Lord, "This day is an impossibility to me. It is going to be simply wonderful to see what You do to get me through it!"

He calmed my panicking spirit and gave me a peace that everything would be done and on time.

As I typed that afternoon, I was suddenly conscious of the fact that I was feeding the machine paper and was hardly aware of the typing each page required. My fingers were flying over the keyboard.

Shortly before the supper hour, I stopped typing and gave the house a quick vacuuming. After the meeting, I finished the typing – and before midnight!

The Lord is so good! If I had become frantic (which was the natural thing to do), I would have been slowed down with errors and confusion. But He provided the calm He had promised and performed a miracle, as far as I was concerned.

Try it sometime. Try patience instead of panic, trust instead of frustration, confidence instead of confusion. The text above is a promise from the One who can provide that quietness of heart in the midst of the roaring tempest.

Thy will be done

Bible Reading: John 14:26-27

I will pray the Father, and he shall give you another
Comforter, that he may abide with you for ever; ...
I will not leave you comfortless: I will come to you.
John 14:16-18

One of our Bible school students received word that her father was dying. It was a shock. Her father had been active, vibrant, and apparently in the best of health. He was only in his fifties. Why should the Lord be taking him home so soon? Why wouldn't he be allowed to keep on, active in Christian work and faithful in missionary support? What would they do without their devoted father and husband?

After the funeral Dorothy wrote us this note:

"The Lord worked and timed everything perfectly, so

even my older brother was able to be home from Africa to see Dad before he died and to be at the funeral.

"The Lord's grace and strength have been sufficient at this time as He has promised.

"A clear salvation message was given at Dad's funeral, and this resulted in many opportunities to witness for Christ. Many of Dad's business associates came and asked questions."

And her mother wrote:

"His homegoing has been quite a shock to me; however, I do not question the Lord as to why He took him. Through this ordeal I have experienced the sustaining grace of the Lord, and praise Him for all He has done for me."

Each of us has her own time of trial and grief to bear. How does sorrow affect us? Does it get us down, burden us day and night, or do we say, "Thy will be done, Father. I will not question why."

Oh, don't misunderstand me! Sorrow is a terribly real and heavy burden. It is indeed natural to feel keenly the loss of a loved one: the emptiness and loneliness which he leaves behind, the many reminders that stab our hearts and bring tears to our eyes. These reactions are not wrong.

But our loving heavenly Father gives us His Comforter to sustain us, to make endurable those days of heavy trial.

The rain is worth it!

Bible Reading: 2 Corinthians 4:15-18

For our light affliction, which is but for a moment, worketh for us a far more exceeding and eternal weight of glory (v. 17).

Stevie was returning home from running an errand when it suddenly started raining, a real downpour. Although only a block from home when it began, he arrived soaked. After shedding his dripping jacket and shoes and drying his face and hair, he stood by the window watching the rain. As unexpectedly as it had started, it stopped.

"The sun is shining," Stevie announced; and I could see the reflection on the wall. Then I heard shouts of joy. "A rainbow! No, it's a double rainbow! Oh, Dad, come see! The rain is worth it – just for the rainbow!" We all ran to the windows. And there it was, a brilliant double arch of color against the steel gray sky.

I thought of that rainbow again next morning when I was speaking with an acquaintance. She confided how precious the Lord had been to her family during the past few months of trials and uncertainty.

Without the rain we would miss the glorious beauty of the rainbow. Without times of testing and difficulty we might have missed the nearness, the dearness of the Lord.

The beauty of the rainbow makes the inconvenience of the rain of little consequence. The preciousness of our heavenly Father makes the trials of life bearable, in fact, well-worth the trouble they have caused.

When David faced stormy trials, he was able to write, "One thing have I desired of the Lord ... to behold the beauty of the Lord" (Psalm 27:4).

I am praying, blessed Saviour,
For a faith so clear and bright,
That its eye will see Thy glory
Through the deepest, darkest night..
~ Fanny J. Crosby ~

Treasures of honey

Bible Reading: 1 Timothy 6:6-21

*But ten men were found among them that said unto
Ishmael, Slay us not: for we have treasures in the field,
of wheat, and of barley, and of oil, and of honey.*
Jeremiah 41:8

When preaching sermons, my husband usually sticks
pretty close to the expository type of message. But
recently he surprised his congregation by announcing
that he was speaking on "*How to Prepare for the Coming
Crash* – in the Light of Scripture."

What had prompted this diversion was his reading of
Robert Preston's popular book, *How to Prepare for the
Coming Crash*. It is, of course, speaking of the financial
crash that some economists are predicting for our
continent.

Dealing with what people should do to prepare for the

crash, the author makes very specific suggestions for the protection of any wealth a person may have accumulated. And then he strongly advocates the storing of extra food and water supplies to carry a family through an emergency. He carefully lists what foods keep well, which are especially nutritious, and how much is required for each individual for a given amount of time.

Certainly it is up to each person what preparations, if any, he chooses to make for any coming emergencies. But for the Christian, our most valuable treasures are ones which cannot be affected by any kind of "crash". God's promises cannot be taken from us; they cannot devaluate; they cannot be stolen; they cannot be exhausted; they cannot wear out.

Our treasures, sure and lasting, are hidden in the honey of God's Word. These treasures can be stored in our hearts for any time of trial, be it personal or international.

Keep on praying

Bible Reading: Ephesians 6:10-20

*Praying always with all prayer and supplication
in the Spirit, and watching thereunto with all
perseverance and supplication for all saints (v. 18).*

One summer it was our privilege to visit with some of
our missionaries working in another country. For the
first time we got a little glimpse of what it is like to
work on a foreign mission field.

There was the language barrier. It was impossible to
ask a single question or get a simple direction. We also
witnessed the disappointment of a new missionary who
had failed her course in this new language.

There was the unfamiliar currency: the frustration of
needing to buy an article and not knowing which coins
to produce, let alone whether or not one was getting
proper value from his money!

There was the inefficient service (at least by North American standards). For example, we had to wait in a long line to get currency exchanged, with the wicket ahead closed – even though it was supposed to be open.

There was the natural reserve of the people and their determination to remain aloof. Our missionary friend remarked that one day he had opened the garage door for his neighbour. Out jumped the man, shouting, determined to find the motive behind such kindness.

Personally, I think I found it harder to accept this different culture because the surroundings seemed similar to what we are used to. The people looked like us; they had houses and apartments much the same as ours. Yet everything was changed.

I left, feeling that I had a bit better idea how to pray for missionaries, not just those who have been on the field for years and years (they most certainly need our continued prayers) but also for new missionaries during their months and years of adjustments. Pray that the Lord will keep them there and help with all the frustrations they must face daily.

Crowns are not for sharing

Bible Reading: 1 Corinthians 3:5-15

*Every man shall receive his own reward
according to his own labour (v. 8).*

After I had finished telling the Bible story to my beginner class, each child started making a crown as a handwork project.

First, they were to color brightly the "jewels". One little girl we'll call Sally was very determined to get hold of the scissors and fix her crown up right! All my coaxing couldn't dissuade her. Her crown was soon in pieces.

As the other children completed their crowns, and I helped fit them to their heads, it became obvious to Sally

78

that she wouldn't have a crown to wear. Next thing I knew, she was kneeling down beside her bench silently sobbing.

After a few moments passed, her brother (about a year older) noticed Sally. Slipping over, he knelt down beside her, sweetly put his arm around her shoulder, and soothingly said, "Don't cry. I'll let you wear my crown part of the time."

Of course, Sally's crown was only a construction paper crown. But how will it be when we get to heaven? Will we find that we have ruined our chances of receiving a crown by taking matters into our own hands, by trying to run our own lives? It won't be possible then for some loving relative or friend to offer to share his crown with us. It just won't work! What we do with our lives here on earth will determine the rewards we will receive when we get to heaven.

Take up thy cross, and follow on,
Nor think till death to lay it down;
For only he who bears the cross
May hope to wear the glorious crown.
~ Charles W. Everest ~

Afterward it yieldeth

Bible Reading: Hebrews 12:6-11

Now no chastening for the present seemeth to be joyous, but grievous: nevertheless afterward it yieldeth the peaceable fruit of righteousness unto them which are exercised thereby (v. 11).

Not one of my fingers is green – let alone my thumb! My family and friends could relate story after story of beautiful, green, thriving plants arriving at our home simply to go the way of all other plants that have visited us for their short doomed stay.

Oh, no, it is not that I don't like plants. I enjoy them very, very much – for the first few days when they are lush and luxuriant. And it is difficult not to envy people who are so successful with them. It will always remain a mystery concerning why they come to such a fate in my house. Is it the way I look at them? Perhaps the way

I talk to them – or don't talk to them?

Anyway, a few weeks ago another plant was headed the way of all the others. What a sick, spindly looking sight! Already I had moved it to a room where it wouldn't be seen by visitors! In one last desperate effort I took our cutting scissors and cut and cut and cut. There wasn't much left, but I at least had the satisfaction of having tried!

And I just can't believe it! The remaining stem is now growing lots of tiny leaves.

Sometimes the One who tends the garden of our lives finds it necessary to remove branch after branch, perhaps all different shapes and sizes of branches. It hurts; it leaves us feeling lonely and forsaken. But we shouldn't get bitter or feel discouraged. There is then room for new leaves and fruit, for new life, new spiritual life.

You know why
we don't know

Bible Reading: James 1:1-12

The trying of your faith worketh patience (v. 3).

As Monica stood at her ironing board, she was thinking of the future. It seemed so uncertain. Why, she wondered, wasn't the Lord answering their prayers and revealing to them the next step? They had been praying long and fervently, and yet they were thoroughly confused concerning their future.

Could it be that God was trying to teach them something through the delay? Could it be that He wasn't ready yet for them to know more than they already knew?

Suddenly, Monica set down her iron, looked out the window before her at the snow-laden trees, and exclaimed aloud, "Thank You, Lord! Thank You that You know the future, and thank You that You know why we don't know it!"

An unspeakable peace surged through her. Now she was confident that God knew what He was doing, even though she had no way of knowing what it was. It simply wasn't His time yet for her to know.

Let us put our faith and trust in our perfect Guide. We can depend on Him, even when circumstances baffle us. He has promised that He won't fail us. Oh, maybe He will test our patience, but He knows what He is doing, and He knows why He is doing it.

Let's claim the promise given in Psalm 48:14: "For this God is our God for ever and ever: he will be our guide even unto death." With perfect confidence we can then face the future.

How sweet, my Saviour, to repose
On Thine almighty power!
To feel Thy strength upholding me
Thro' every trying hour!

Why should my heart then be distressed
By dread of future ill?
Or why should unbelieving fear
My trembling spirit fill?
~ Caesar Malan ~

We love you

Bible Reading: 1 Corinthians 13:1-13

*Let us consider one another to provoke
unto love and to good works.*
Hebrews 10:24

$\mathcal{I}$ had been putting hours of work and preparation into wedding plans for a friend.

The day arrived, and I was miserable, not germsick, but sore and achy from having dislocated my left shoulder the day before. After having the shoulder reset, I really had no choice but to continue with my duties. Thankfully, the helpers were most co-operative, but I had the responsibility. Admittedly, the hours seemed like days.

Finally, I was on my way home and very much looking forward to getting into a horizontal position. My husband wouldn't be there. I knew he had had to leave the wedding a bit early to attend another appointment.

After entering the house, I walked through the kitchen on my way to the bedroom. Propped up on the table was a note in Ted's handwriting. It said simply, "We love you."

My spirits revived! Of course, I knew my husband and boys loved me, but his sweet thoughtfulness in bothering to leave a note to tell me so really was a boost.

I still have this note, and I intend to keep it. It speaks to me of the kindnesses that cost so little materially yet are so encouraging along life's weary way.

It would add a cheery note to all our households if we would sometimes go out of our way to do that little extra bit or express in words what we have been thinking but assumed the other person knows.

Our God is love; and all his saints
His image bear below;
The heart with love to God inspired,
With love to man will glow.
~ Thomas Cotterill ~

Add wings to your prayers

Bible Reading: Philippians 2:1-12

*Work out your own salvation
with fear and trembling (v. 12).*

Chocolate-chip cookies were Charlotte's favorites. Her mother tried to keep them on hand, but today the cookie jar was empty.

"Please make some cookies, Mommie," begged the three-year-old.

"Oh, honey, I'm nearly out of sugar. I can't go to the store today. This house has to be cleaned!"

"But, Mommie, I want some chocolate-chip cookies," Charlotte persisted.

"I know, dear. Just run and play now. I'll make some tomorrow."

Mother returned to her cleaning in the front part of

the house. Unknown to her, Charlotte climbed a chair, knelt on the counter top, and took a cup from the cupboard.

Clutching the cup, she slipped out across the lawn to the neighbor's house.

Holding out the cup, she didn't hesitate, "Mommie needs to borrow some sugar, please."

To the neighbor's inquiry as to how much was wanted, Charlotte didn't have an answer.

But she got her sugar. Triumphant Charlotte marched home. The sound of the vacuum led her to her mother. Hugging her treasure, she announced, "Now you can make some chocolate-chip cookies!"

Prayer is an important ingredient in a Christian's life. The disciples implored the Lord Jesus to teach them to pray. This He did.

And God delights in answering our prayers. But sometimes maybe He wants to use us to help answer the prayers we have been praying for others.

Perhaps He has given us all we require to take care of some need ourselves. Then it is not sufficient only to pray. Do something. Add "wings" to your prayers, as Charlotte did.

The words haunted him

Bible Reading: James 1:19-26

He that is soon angry dealeth foolishly ... He that is slow to wrath is of great understanding.
Proverbs 14:17,29

Norman was the victim of an unhappy childhood. His parents called themselves Christians, and probably they were; but his father had an uncontrollable temper.

Norman says he vividly recalls the evening his father was locking up their small grocery store. As his father turned the lock, Norman remembered having left inside the bag of groceries his mother had ordered.

Fearfully, he told his father of his forgetfulness.

Unlocking the door, the father shouted and scolded in an outburst of anger, but the phrase that still lingers in Norman's mind is, "I wish you had never been born."

Norman remembers going home, shutting himself in

his closet, and sobbing. His father wished he hadn't ever been born! He wished it, too, but there was nothing he could do about it! His ten-year-old heart ached.

Probably Norman's father never thought again about the cruel words he had spoken. He was used to blurting out harsh statements in his uncontrolled moments. But Norman never forgot. The words haunted him.

We cannot control our tempers by ourselves. We need to give them over to God, give them back to Him to control. Our unguarded words may wound one of our dear children for life even though we may not really have meant what we said.

Angry words! O let them never
From the tongue unbridled slip;
May the heart's best impulse ever
Check them ere they soil the lip.

Love is much too pure and holy,
Friendship is too sacred far,
For a moment's reckless folly
Thus to desolate and mar.

Angry words are lightly spoken,
Bitterest thoughts are rashly stirred,
Brightest links of life are broken,
By a single angry word.
~ Horatio R. Palmer ~

I can't get it out of my mind!

Bible Reading: Psalm 119:9-16

Thy word have I hid in mine heart, that
I might not sin against Thee (v. 11).

Our eight-year-old came home from school – starving, as usual. Getting out the can of peanut butter, a knife, and the loaf of bread, he prepared himself a sandwich. I noticed the peanut butter spread a little thicker than I would have done it. But I said nothing. I didn't want to squelch this streak of independence!

Nearly half the sandwich was down by the time I had poured Davie a glass of milk.

Between bites, he suddenly burst out, "'O sing unto the Lord a new song: sing unto the Lord, all the earth.'

That's Psalm 96:1. I can't get it out of my mind."

And then he continued to repeat it a few more times. His mouth full of peanut-butter sandwich didn't seem to slow him down!

I began thinking. How lovely to be able to remember God's Word! About what else would I rather have Davie say, "I can't get it out of my mind"?

Again I silently thanked God for the privilege of having our children attend a Christian grade school, where they are taught God's Word as part of the day's learning.

Every child cannot attend Christian schools, but all our children can be memorizing God's Word, tucking it away so firmly that they won't be able to get it out of their minds in the days and years to come.

And what is good for our children is good for us. Are there special portions that speak to you? Commit each one to memory so thoroughly that you can truly say, "I can't get it out of my mind."

That's all it takes

Bible Reading: Matthew 10:40-42

*Whosoever shall give you a cup of water to
drink in my name, because ye belong to Christ,
verily I say unto you, he shall not lose his reward.*
Mark 9:41

*H*ard as it is to believe, the plant I mentioned is still
alive and flourishing! But, not without a struggle!

The other day I noticed all the leaves sagging and
hanging limply. How sad and dejected it looked! Having
attained an unusual height (for a plant of mine), its
planter is proving too small. Besides that, it is sitting in
a window where the hot sunshine beats on it.

Poking at the earth, I found it hard as rocks. Quickly I
poured on some snow water, and in a few hours the plant
looked like new. No longer were the leaves drooping;

they were holding their purple-and-green faces high.

Just a fraction of a cup of water had made all the difference.

Have you ever passed someone on the walk who looks like a wilted plant? You know immediately something is wrong. Her face is long; her spirit is sagging. Take time to give a smile and a cheery greeting.

Or maybe someone phones. You are desperately rushed. Yet you sense there is a need, a need for her to know you care enough to spend a few minutes chatting with her.

Or perhaps someone arrives at your door just as you are ready to dash out to work on the list of errands you have carefully arranged for the day. But she needs someone with whom to talk and share her burdens. You take off your coat, forget the list, and concentrate on lifting her load.

Maybe the cup of water mentioned in our scripture portion can be given in more ways than we realize at first. Encouragement given to the discouraged can have as dramatic an effect as water poured on a sad-looking plant! That's all it takes.

She was real grumpy!

Bible Reading: 2 Corinthians 3:1-6

*The epistle of Christ, ... written not with ink,
but with the Spirit of the living God (v. 3).*

Our boys lay sprawled on the kitchen floor, passing the holiday hours quietly for a change. Before them were some pictures of days gone by. I was working at the sink and couldn't help overhearing their comments as they turned the pages.

Eventually they came to a picture of someone I thought neither of them would remember. But to my surprise I heard Stevie saying, "Oh, I remember her! That's — . She was real grumpy!"

I didn't rebuke him for his frankness. After all, I wasn't supposed to be in on their conversation. And I did have to admit that there was a great deal of truth to what he

94

said. Even a very young boy had noted an undesirable aspect in the character of this lady.

But I didn't go on thinking of the lady and her obvious faults. I began thinking about myself. "What," I asked, "would a child in his blunt honesty say when he came across my picture?"

We may not be conscious that our everyday lives are making an impression on anyone. And an impression for impression's sake is not important. Paul could write to the Corinthian Christians that their lives had made an impression for Christ. He could say of them that they were recognized as being true Christians by the way they lived.

Let us seek to be such living letters.

Whatever you do, wherever you go,
Be loyal to Jesus, your King!
Oh, serve Him aright, and walk in the light:
Be loyal to Jesus, your King!
~ Ida Scott Taylor ~

Squeaks and scratches

Bible Reading: Psalm 51:9-13

*Create in me a clean heart, O God; and
renew a right spirit within me (v. 10).*

It was another of those hot windy days. The plant world
was crying for rain. The gardens were dry; the flowers
looked parched and thirsty; some of the grass was turning
an ugly yellowish brown.

Once or twice a day an extra strong gust of wind swept
across the prairies, bringing with it a cloud of dust and
dirt. Whenever I heard one of these coming, I dashed
around trying to get the windows and doors shut in time.
It wasn't always possible.

To add to our dust problem, construction work was
being done across the street. Large trucks and heavy
equipment continually stirred up the black earth. But it

was too hot to keep the house closed tight. We would just have to put up with it.

At supper my husband came home from the office. As is his usual custom, he walked over to the record player to put on some music. To his dismay he discovered that some of the records he had left on at noon were scratched. The particles of dust which had sifted into the house were ground into the records by the needle.

Only tiny specks of dust, but they ruined the perfect sound of the records. Yes, we could still hear the music, but it was in addition to the squeaks and scratches.

I was reminded of how precious little it takes to ruin the sweet music of our lives. Just a tiny speck of something miserable can mar the harmony that we as Christians should be exhibiting. It doesn't take much, and it doesn't take long, but the damage is permanent.

Too much honey

Bible Reading: Proverbs 16:18-19

*It is not good to eat much honey: so for
men to search their own glory is not glory.*
Proverbs 25:27

We were enjoying the gracious company of one of
our guest conference speakers. During the meal he kept
us entertained with his stories. Then, not really meaning
to, he told us of an experience he had had with honey.

Some years ago he had decided that for the sake of
keeping fit and finding sufficient energy for his vigorous
round of meetings, he would eat honey. And he did! As
he would study in his hotel room between meetings, he
would consume tea and honey. Every chance he had, he
ate honey. He had been sure that honey was a good health
food, and he had done nothing to limit his intake of it.

Suddenly, one day he found himself a very sick man. Rushed to the hospital, he was examined by the doctors. It was discovered that his body was having a reaction to all the honey he had been eating. He was nearly diabetic!

Now honey is a good food. Honey-and-peanut-butter sandwiches are a regular order around our home! But as our friend learned the hard way, one can get too much of it.

The gentleman himself confessed that if he had read his Bible properly, he should have really known better!

Praise is also sweet, and we all need a certain measure of praise and approval to function at our best. On the other hand, however, we should not covet continually the praise of others. As our verse for today tells us, when we ask for appreciation, it really isn't true thanks that is given. The person giving the commendation is doing so only because he feels obligated to do so.

Let us then be content with any bit of appreciation that may be sinerely shown, remembering that this once or twice is better for us than an overdose of insincere praise that may give us a false and devastating pride.

Ugly clods in my garden

Bible Reading: Hosea 10:12-15

For thus saith the Lord to the men of Judah and Jerusalem, Break up your fallow ground, and sow not among thorns.
Jeremiah 4:3

Isaiah the prophet says that a garden causes "the things that are sown in it to spring forth" (Isaiah 61:11). Ours certainly did so one year, except for a part of the garden. Let me tell you about it.

After our garden was plowed that spring, I had an urge to start planting my seeds! When could I begin? I went out to look it over. To my dismay, hard clods were everywhere. Planting a garden is one thing, but raking one full of lumps is quite another.

That settled it! I asked a strong lad to do the raking for

me. He set out energetically. Soon he returned to say he had finished.

As I looked over the fence, I saw the hardest clods, which could not be broken, in a long neat row about two thirds down the garden. Reading my thoughts, the fellow explained that the garden dipped there and so he had filled it with the clods. I didn't have the heart to ask him to drag them to the side.

"Oh, well," I reasoned, "When it rains, the lumps will break up. What's the difference?"

So I thought! As the plants started growing, I noticed a bare spot in every row about two-thirds down and about two feet wide. As the weeks passed, some of the seeds did start to grow, but they were obviously behind the rest. The clods had all disintegrated, but their effect was lasting.

Clods – hard, unwielding balls of earth – do not contribute to a bountiful harvest either in the vegetable garden or in the garden of our hearts. There may be a few hard lumps we are hanging on to, confident they won't affect our testimony. But they do! Their presence will soon be obvious to those about us if we don't get rid of them now.

Especially carrots

Bible Reading: 1 Corinthians 12:1-12

*And there are diversities of operations, but it
is the same God which worketh all in all (v. 6).*

$\mathcal{A}$s we drove home with friends from our country
church, we spent the time discussing the morning service.
Ted had been continuing his series of messages on the
gifts of the Spirit, and he had been emphasizing the part
each of us must play in the proper functioning of the
church.

After we had walked in our front door, I exclaimed,
"I wish I knew what my talent is. Maybe then I wouldn't
be so torn between trying to do umpteen different jobs."

Our eleven-year-old son, who was only half listening,
piped up, "You have lots of talents, Mom." After listening what he considered to be talents, he concluded, "and

cooking. Oh, maybe not cooking so much! Especially carrots."

It won't be necessary to try to guess who thinks he doesn't like cooked carrots! Let's just think about what we can learn from what Stevie said.

Do we consider other's talents worthy of recognition only if it always involves something that will benefit us? Do we discount someone else's talents just because they are not used exactly as we think they should be?

God has given us our talents. We are responsible to Him for the way we make use of them – or don't make use of them.

O, let us all endeavour, with
all our hearts and might,
To serve our Lord and Master,
and in His work delight;
Remembering that service
must come before reward;
That joy must flow from doing
the Father's will and word.
~ W.B. Williams ~

Cut down – but growing!

Bible Reading: Isaiah 27:1-6

*The house of Judah shall again take root
downward, and bear fruit upward.*
Isaiah 37:31

On a beautiful hot summer day I set out for the campus
proper with a list of errands in my hand.

Approaching the north part of the office building, I
noticed the surrounding walks littered with boards, nails,
tar paper, and other construction supplies. The workmen
were erecting an addition to the administration building.

Having to be careful where I stepped, I was watching
the walk more closely than usual. Suddenly I stopped.
Before me was the stump of a tree that had been cut off
flush with the sidewalk. But all around the stump were
shoots about three or four inches high.

104

Maybe the men, looking down from their ladders, wondered what I was staring at in the middle of the sidewalk. But it intrigued me. A stump which I thought was dead was growing little shoots – lots of them!

Just like Job says in 14:7-9, "For there is hope of a tree, if it be cut down, that it will sprout again, and that the tender branch thereof will not cease. Though the root thereof wax old in the earth, and the stock thereof die in the ground; Yet through the scent of water it will bud, and bring forth boughs like a plant."

Sometimes in the trials of life we get "cut down," as it were. All plants for a useful future are removed. But if our roots are in God, we shall survive every ordeal and, "like a tree planted by the rivers of water," shall bear fruit again.

Be a brother – not a boss

Bible Reading: 1 Peter 5:1-4

*Brethren, if a man be overtaken in a fault,
ye which are spiritual, restore such an
one in the spirit of meekness; conside-
ring thyself, lest thou also be tempted.*
Galatians 6:1

$\mathcal{J}$ had called our boys. I knew they were tired; they had been out late the night before.

Finding it hard to get out of bed myself after a late night probably makes me a bit too sympathetic. I call the boys gently. If they have not stirred, I return a few minutes later trying to think of something interesting to talk about. Maybe it's, "The ground is covered with snow; you should see it!" or "Today you have P.E." or "Remember what we are going to do after school today?"

By the time I have talked for a bit they are usually awake and entering into the conversation, and it is not nearly so hard to get out of that comfy bed.

Anyway, today was a bit different. I had tried my usual tactics. They had worked with Stevie, but Davie was lingering.

The third time I returned, Stevie was dressing and trying to persuade his brother to do the same.

Upon seeing me, Davie exclaimed, "Stevie can't make me dress. He's my brother, not my boss."

After making sure he knew who was his boss and what she wanted, I had time to do some thinking.

In the Christian church we must recognize the brother-to-brother relationship. There is never a place for a boss-servant aspect. Even the elders in 1 Peter 5 are commanded not to lord it over God's flock.

How many difficult situations might be avoided if people spoke as brother to brother and sister to sister, rather than commanding.

If we have to rebuke a fellow Christian, we are told in Galatians 6:1 that we are to go meekly – as a brother, not as a boss!

Yale key must fit yale lock!

Bible Reading: 2 Timothy 2:14-15

Study to shew thyself approved unto God,
a workman that needeth not to be ashamed,
rightly dividing the word of truth (v. 15).

Davie was playing with a string of odd keys. I had borrowed my mother's collection of nearly a hundred to see if I could find a key to fit a certain lock.

Before I returned the keys, however, Davie was playing with them, trying them out in the doors of our house.

As he tried key after key in our front door, he was becoming a bit perplexed. Finally, he spoke his thoughts aloud, "Yale key must fit Yale lock." But it didn't! Indeed, it was a Yale key and a Yale lock, but these particular ones were not meant to match.

There are people who just grab any verse from the

Bible to apply to any situation. Trying to apply the wrong verse to a given problem only leads to frustration. It is the part of wisdom to be able to provide the right Bible solution to the problem, not to just open your Bible and point to a verse and take that for guidance.

Probably the Lord has overruled our ignorance and has sometimes seen fit to answer in this manner. But wouldn't it be better to get to know the Scriptures well enough to give us an overall background for the decisions we have to make?

May our prayer be that of the psalmist who declared, "I have not departed from thy judgments: for thou hast taught me ... Through thy precepts I get understanding ... Thy word is a lamp unto my feet, and a light unto my path" (Psalm 119:102,104,105).

Thanks for Thy Word, O blessed Redeemer!
Open our eyes its beauty to see;
Grant us Thy grace to study it wisely,
Close every heart to all but Thee.
~ Fanny J. Crosby ~

Standing on your mountain

Bible Reading: Joshua 14:6-15

Now, therefore give me this mountain (v. 12).

Stevie bounded in the door.

"Hey, Mom," he shouted, "We had the most fun at recess this morning on a mountain of snow. The fourth and fifth grade boys were playing out there, pushing each other down the hill." I hoped it was safer than it sounded!

But the next thing I knew Stevie was changing his socks. The story leaked out. As they were playing, quite a quantity of snow had filled his boots; and when it was time to come home for dinner, he could pour the water out of them. Naturally his socks, too, were well soaked by the time he reached home.

I remonstrated. "You'll have to find something else to wear this afternoon. Your boots won't be dry." With that we dropped the subject and had dinner.

As Stevie prepared to leave for school, I poked my head around the corner. "What do you have on your feet?"

I didn't need a reply. There he stood in boots at least three inches longer than his feet. "You can't waddle to school in those!" I exclaimed.

"They are okay. They will help me stand on the mountain." Now, if I had been the one to suggest he wear such boots! Oh, well!

Oversized boots good for standing on a mountain! It reminds me of what Caleb said to Joshua in our scripture portion for today. Sometimes you may think you need an oversize dose of faith to trust God in the midst of the circumstances you face. Ask Him for it! He will help you stand on your mountain!

Out of the fog

Bible Reading: Job 23:1-17

*For it is God which worketh in you both
to will and to do of his good pleasure.
Philippians 2:13*

$\mathcal{E}$xplaining hoarfrost to a person who has never seen it is something like telling the Eskimos what a heat wave is!

At any rate, we had hoarfrost – lots of it! For about five days our part of sunny Alberta was enclosed in fog. It would, of course, lift a bit in the daytime, but not enough to let us see the sun. And at night it descended upon us, enveloping the world with its eerie gray shadows.

But the fog brought something very beautiful: hoarfrost. We had no snow on the ground, only hoarfrost, a

112

thick, lacy, sparkling coating of pure white ice particles. It had turned all our sourroundings into a wonderland of beauty.

The bare branches were coated with a layer of hoarfrost hanging from them. The telephone lines hung low under the weight of their beautiful burden. Roadside weeds became dainty white ferns. Even telephone and fence posts were plastered with this transforming hoarfrost.

It was breath-taking to view. There were no ugly or bare places left in its path. Our little world was one complete exquisite picture.

But if we had had the sun, we wouldn't have had the hoarfrost. The fog and the dampness and darkness of the night brought the beauty.

Do we complain and rebel when all about us seems dark and depressing? Do our trials and testings get us down? Do we look only at the fog, the troubles? Maybe our Maker sees we need the dark hours to create within us a beauty we could not otherwise obtain. Let us trust Him that out of the depths of our night His likeness will be formed in us.

Your heavenly Father knoweth

Bible Reading: Matthew 6:28-34

O ye of little faith ... your heavenly Father knoweth
that ye have need of all these things (vv. 30,32).

*G*race and her husband make it a practice to dole out each month's pay check into envelopes, ready for the bills when they arrive.

On the evening before moving, they were hustling about doing last-minute jobs. In the mail had come their electric bill. They would run the money down to their landlady, requesting her to pay the bill. But, alas! Upon opening the envelope marked "Hydro Bill," Grace found nothing. The money was gone!

Grace's husband confessed to having forgotten to tell

her that he had needed the money for gas and school supplies. She felt bewildered, not so much because her husband had forgotten to tell her but because the money simply wasn't there for the debt. What could she do? Grace told the Lord, "We have been giving You our tithe; You will have to do something about this." Would the Lord be interested in an electric bill?

A little while later they went downstairs to say good-bye to their landlady and took along money borrowed from another fund to give her to pay their electric bill.

As they chatted, their Christian landlady told them that instead of giving them ten dollars, which she made a practice of giving tenants when they left, she wanted to pay their electric bill.

So this was what God was doing – testing Grace and all the while planning to supply this urgent need. The landlady knew nothing of their dilemma, but God did!

Is God interested in the little details that make up daily living? Of course, He is concerned about the big crises, but His concern doesn't end there. Let us trust in God's faithfulness.

Praise Him, all ye people

Bible Reading: Psalm 105:1-5

*O praise the Lord, all ye nations: praise him,
all ye people. For his merciful kindness is
great toward us: and the truth of the Lord
endureth for ever. Praise ye the Lord.*
Psalm 117

$\mathcal{M}$rs. F. had been struggling all day long with her sewing machine. She had tried this setting and that setting, but she just couldn't get the tension right. Becoming more and more frustrated, she didn't know what to do. She badly needed her sewing machine to sew properly.

Still by late afternoon she had not succeeded. To rest her eyes and her aching head, she left the machine to pick up their mail. In the box was *The Prairie Overcomer*, which she decided to look at before returning to the problems of her sewing machine.

In that issue I had written concerning the way the Lord had answered prayer to make our washing machine work.

She says she just decided that if the Lord could make my washing machine wash, He could make her sewing machine sew. So she prayed.

And, you know, the Lord was pleased to answer her prayer. He helped her fix the tension properly, and the machine sewed beautifully!

Sometimes we may be reluctant to share with others the specific answers to prayer we experience. But I believe that sometimes God wants us to do so in order to strengthen not only our faith but also the faith of others. After all, He who hears and answers us is certainly worthy of our praise.

Now, in a song of grateful praise,
To my dear Lord my voice I'll raise;
With all His saints I'll join to tell,
My Jesus has done all things well!
~ Samuel Medley ~

My Bible is cold!

Bible Reading: Psalm 119:41-48

*Continue thou in the things which thou hast
learned and hast been assured of, knowing
of whom thou hast learned them.*
2 Timothy 3:14

Supper was finished, and the dishes were stacked. As is our habit, we then proceeded into the living room. It was time for family devotions.

But Davie couldn't find his Bible. He ran off to look in his bedroom. Maybe he had left it there. Soon he returned empty-handed. Where could his Bible be?

Knowing that nothing could be very far away in our tiny house, I questioned, "Where did you have it last, Davie?"

He thought, then brightened. "I took it to church. But

118

I'm sure I brought it home. Maybe it is still in the car."

Thus saying, he was out the door, forgetting that it was far too wintry for even a quick dash without extra clothing.

In a moment he was back, shivering and clutching his precious Bible. Having wiped his feet, he crossed the rug to me. Hoping for a noisy reaction, he held his Bible against my arm and exclaimed, "My Bible is *cold*." Was it ever!

Since then I've not been able to get that phrase out of my mind, "My Bible is cold."

True, in Davie's case it was simply a matter of the elements. But other things can cause our Bibles to seem cold to us. Neglect is one sure way to lose interest in the Word of God. Disobedience and sin can also cause our Bibles to seem cold. Is my Bible cold? If it is, why?

Great God, with wonder and with praise
On all Thy works I look!
But still Thy wisdom, power, and grace,
Shine brightest in Thy Book.

Then may I love my Bible more,
And take a fresh delight
By day to read these wonders o'er,
And meditate by night.
~ Isaac Watts ~

For show or for service?

Bible Reading: Revelation 3:19-22

It was noised that he was in [my] house.
Mark 2:1

$\mathcal{A}$t one of our spring missionary conferences, one of the speakers told of a lady in whose luxurious house he had stayed while in Australia. As he was preparing to leave the home, he noticed his hostess busily covering her plush furniture with dust covers.

His curiosity eventually conquered his manners, and he asked her what was going on. She poured out her story.

Some time before, the Lord had spoken to her about giving her house back to Him. It was a long, painful struggle. After all, hadn't she finally managed to furnish it to suit her dreams?

The battle raged. At last she told the Lord He could use her home. Donning her coat and hat, she set out for her pastor's office to tell him that he could announce the next ladies' meeting at her place.

But she hadn't walked far when the Lord stopped her. She was clearly convinced that the ladies' meeting wasn't what the Lord had in mind. What then? No, it couldn't be! "I'm supposed to give my house for children's meetings?"

With this conviction in her heart she yielded and experienced great joy and fruit in obeying her Lord.

Housewife, is your home consecrated to the Lord for Him to use in any way He pleases? Not just for meetings that will not mess up the house but for anything the Lord should want in it. Maybe it is entertaining; maybe it is children's meetings; maybe it is starting a Bible study group among the neighborhood ladies.

Or perhaps He has part of our house, but part of it you are hanging on to. Give Him every room!

Get obeying!

Bible Reading: Luke 6:46-49

*And why call ye me, Lord, Lord, and
do not the things which I say? (v. 46).*

Our family had come in rather late from attending an anniversary celebration. I was attempting to hustle the boys off to bed as quickly as possible. As I sat at the kitchen table finishing up a bit of work, Davie bounded in, half ready for bed. He opened our "what-not" drawer, produced the paper punch, and started punching holes around the sheet of paper. To my dismay he was working over the drawer, and the "confetti" that didn't fall into it was tumbling to the floor.

"Davie, what are you doing? Stop," I commanded. I might as well have been talking to the wall. He determinedly speeded up his hole-punching and didn't answer a word.

Rather taken aback by his outright disobedience, I started toward him to see whatever was so important. He fled, tossing me the paper and explaining, "I had to."

In my hand I held a certificate given him at Sunday school. It read, "I belong to the Obey Your Parents Club." The punched holes were supposed to represent all the times he had obeyed us!

Imagine deliberately disobeying me in order to produce a certificate stating his obedience! But maybe we do that sometimes with God. We say we want to obey Him, even as we continue to do the things we want to do in the way we want to do them. How much better it would be to ease up on our promises and get to obeying!

Have you lost your brains?

Bible Reading: Psalm 71:1-5

*In thee, O Lord, do I put my trust: let
me never be put to confusion (v. 1).*

Monday morning in our home is always an extra-busy one. But this particular Monday was especially hectic. Our neighborhood families were planning a get-together, and somehow I had got myself involved in coordinating the food.

So I was dashing from house to house with notebook and pen in hand, writing down what was needed and who would bring what. Arriving at the last house, I was greeted at the door by the occupant's grandson. Before his mother could say a word, the little fellow blurted out, "Have you lost your brains?" He had been watching out the window!

Having boys of my own, I was not shocked by his question. In fact, I had to agree with him that I must have appeared to be looking for something. But he set me thinking.

As Christmas season again approaches, are we letting ourselves get so busily involved in what we think are necessary preparations that our children wonder if *we* have lost our brains.

I know how it is. That list of "Things to Do Before Christmas" can become overwhelming. But is it all absolutely necessary? What if we make only five kinds of cookies instead of ten? What if we don't get our own new dress sewn? Surely the unruffled, rested, calm mother means more to our children on Christmas Day than all the extras we can dream up. This might even give us opportunity to talk with them more about the real meaning of Christmas.

You need to have Him along

Bible Reading: Matthew 1:18-25

And she shall bring forth a son, and thou
shalt call his name Jesus: for he shall
save his people from their sins (v. 21).

We had just celebrated Stevie's tenth birthday. The last boy had gone home, and I got busy picking up the pieces: doing the dishes, sweeping up crumbs of birthday cake, straightening furniture and throwing away torn wrapping paper.

By the time my husband came home from the office, the house was pretty well restored to order. But our boys didn't want any supper; they were too full of banana splits and cake and candy. After all the noise and excitement of the party, I was glad to let them play while we enjoyed a quiet meal together.

As we were nearing the end of our supper – left overs from the party being a handy dessert – Davie came in. "What are you doing?"

"Oh," I teased, "We are just having a little birthday party for Stevie all on our own."

Davie sobered. "If it is Stevie's birthday party, you need to have him along," he reprimanded.

I smothered a grin. Our literal-minded son would catch that!

But it made me think of all the birthday parties for our Lord Jesus where He isn't along.

We have our elaborate celebrations for the happy Christmas season. We invite our friends and neighbours; we spend hours making our home spotless and ready; we bake and cook all our favorite goodies; we tramp streets and haunt stores for special gifts for our loved ones.

Yet the One whose birthday we honor is absent. Using Davie's words, "If it is Jesus' birthday party, you need to have Him along."